**mommy**

**daddy**

maman

papa

**boy**

**girl**

garçon

fille

*1*
one

un

*2*
two

deux

*3*
three

trois

*4*
four

quatre

**5**

five

cinq

**6**

six

six

**7**

seven

sept

**8**

eight

huit

**9**

nine

neuf

**10**

ten

dix

**count**

**compter**

**write**

**écrire**

**draw**

**dessiner**

**paint**

**peindre**

**circle**

rond

**square**

carré

**rectangle**

rectangle

**triangle**

triangle

**star**

étoile

**black**

noir

**white**

blanc

**brown**

🇫🇷 marron

🇨🇦 brun

**red**

rouge

**blue**

bleu

**yellow**

jaune

**green**

vert

**purple**

violet

**gray**

gris

**orange**

orange

**pink**

rose

**apple**

pomme

**banana**

banane

**pineapple**

ananas

**watermelon**

🇫🇷 pastèque
🇨🇦 melon d'eau

**pear**

poire

**grapes**

raisins

**mango**

mangue

**peach**

pêche

**strawberry**

fraise

**cherry**

cerise

**orange**

orange

**coconut**

noix de coco

**lemon**

citron

**mushroom**

champignon

**corn**

🇫🇷 maïs

🇨🇦 blé d'inde

**tomato**

tomate

**pumpkin**

citrouille

**cucumber**

concombre

**carrot**

carotte

**potato**

🇫🇷 **pomme de terre**
🇨🇦 **patate**

**zucchini**

**courgette**

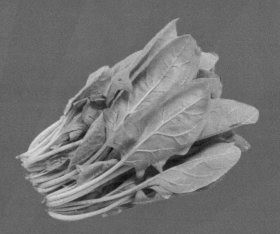

**spinach**

**épinard**

**cauliflower**

**chou-fleur**

**egg**

**oeuf**

**plate**

assiette

**spoon**

cuillère

**knife**

couteau

**fork**

fourchette

**cake**

gâteau

**baby bottle**

biberon

**candies**

bonbons

**cheese**

fromage

**drink**

**boire**

**eat**

**manger**

**hot**

**chaud**

**cold**

**froid**

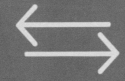 

**small**                          **big**

**petit**                        **grand**

**short**                        **long**

**court**                        **long**

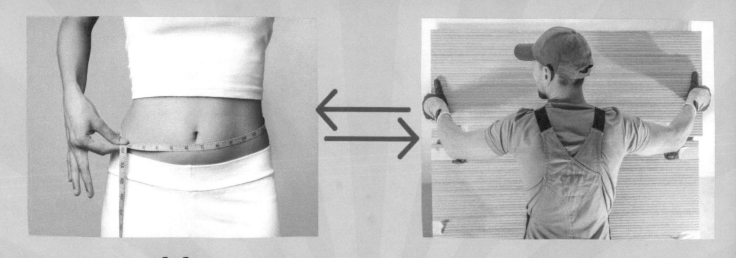

**thin**

mince

**large**

grand

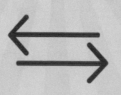

**easy**

facile

**difficult**

difficile

**stand up**

**debout**

**sit down**

**assis**

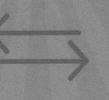

**sweet**

**sucré**

**salty**

**salé**

**heavy**

lourd

**light**

léger

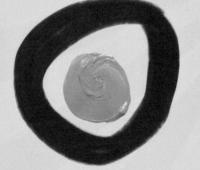

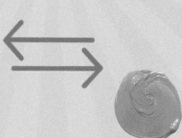

**in**

dedans

**out**

dehors

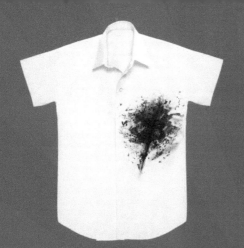

**dirty**

**sale**

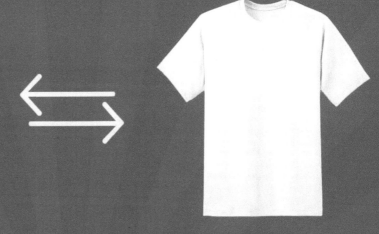

**clean**

**propre**

**close**

**fermé**

**open**

**ouvert**

**pencils**

**crayons**

**clock**

**horloge**

**key**

**clé**

**book**

**livre**

**bed**

lit

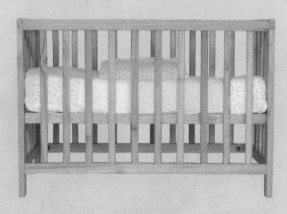

**crib**

lit bébé

**table**

table

**chair**

chaise

## car

🇫🇷 **voiture**
🇨🇦 **char**

## bike

🇫🇷 **vélo**
🇨🇦 **bicyclette**

**plane**

avion

**boat**

bateau

**train**

train

**helicopter**

hélicoptère

**firetruck**

**camion de pompier**

**firefighter**

**pompier**

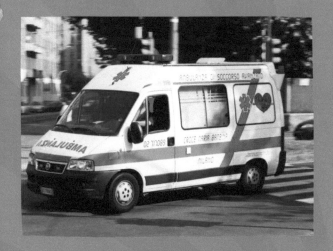

**ambulance**

**ambulance**

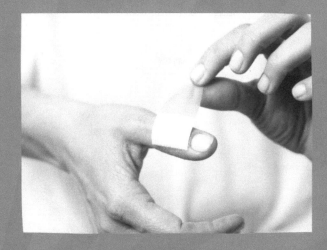

**bandage**

**pansement**

**paramedic**

**ambulancier**

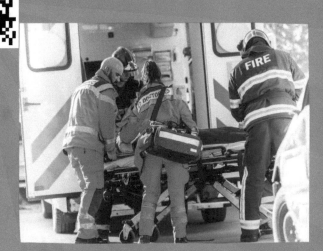

**rescue team**

**équipe de secours**

**forest**

forêt

**mountain**

montagne

**grass**

herbe

**sand**

sable

**tree**

arbre

**flower**

fleur

**butterfly**

papillon

**ant**

fourmi

**cat**

chat

**dog**

chien

**horse**

cheval

**mouse**

souris

**cow**

vache

**pig**

cochon

**sheep**

mouton

**duck**

canard

**goose**

oie

**rabbit**

lapin

**fish**

poisson

**vet**

vétérinaire

**doctor**

docteur

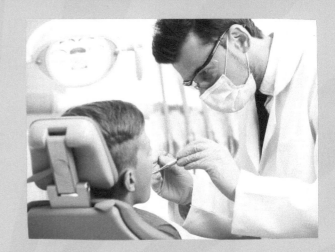

**dentist**

dentiste

**pharmacist**

pharmacien

**nurse**

infirmière

**head**

tête

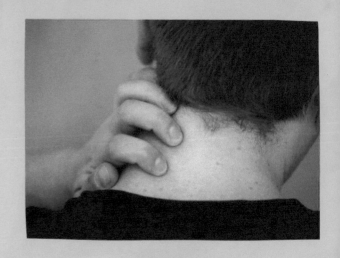

**neck**

cou

**foot**

pied

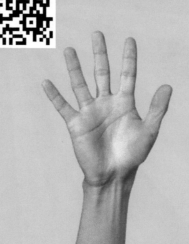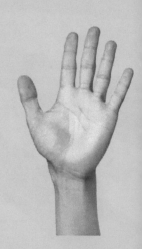

**hand**

main

**teeth**

dents

**eye**

oeil

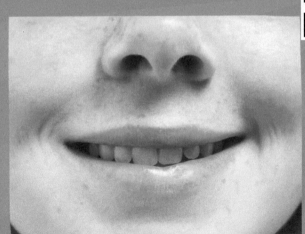

**mouth**

bouche

**ear**

oreille

**hat**

chapeau

**dress**

robe

**pants**

pantalon

**shoes**

🇫🇷 chaussures
🇨🇦 souliers

**coat**

manteau

**scarf**

🇫🇷 **écharpe**
🇨🇦 **foulard**

**umbrella**

parapluie

**glasses**

lunettes

**sun**

soleil

**cloudy**

nuageux

**rainy**

pluvieux

**moon**

lune